LAND THAT I LOVE
Regions of the United States

THE WEST COAST

Niccole Bartley

PowerKiDS press™
New York

Published in 2015 by The Rosen Publishing Group, Inc.
29 East 21st Street, New York, NY 10010

First Edition

Editor: Joanne Randolph
Photo Research: Katie Stryker
Book Design: Colleen Bialecki

Photo Credits: Cover, p 16 (bottom) MariuszBlach/iStock/Thinkstock; pp. 4, 23 Ingram Publishing/Thinkstock; p. 5 Beatrice Preve/Thinkstock; p. 6 Altrendo Nature/Getty Images; p. 7 Bruce Obee/All Canada Photos/Getty Images; p. 8 MPI/Stringer/Archive Photos/Getty Images; p. 9 Stock Montage/Contributor/Archive Photos/Getty Images; p. 10 James L. Amos/Contributor/National Geographic/Getty Images; p. 11 Richard Cummins/Lonely Planet Images/Getty Images; p. 12 Photo By Patrick McManus/Flickr Select/Getty Images; p. 13 Steffi Sawyer/Shutterstock.com; p. 14 tobkatrina/Shutterstock.com; p. 15 Henry Georgi/Aurora/Getty Images; p. 16 (center) Spirit of America/Shutterstock.com; p. 17 (center) nstanev/iStock/Thinkstock; p. 17 (top) Sopotnicki/Shutterstock.com; p. 17 (bottom inset) trekandshoot/Shutterstock.com; p. 17 (top inset) MedioImages/Photodisc; p. 18 Dan Moore/iStock/Thinkstock; p. 19 Anna-Mari West/Shutterstock; p. 20 Monkey Business Images/Thinkstock; p. 21 (top) Mars Lasar/iStock/Thinkstock; p. 21 (inset) 4thegrapes/iStock/Thinkstock; p. 21 (bottom) Ron Wurzer/Stringer/Getty Images News/Getty Images; pp. 16 (top), 24 Thinkstock/Stockbyte; p 25 Purestock/Thinkstock; p. 26 Mark Payne/iStock/Thinkstock; p. 27 Zack Schnepf/iStock/Thinkstock; p. 28 Greg Epperson/iStock/Thinkstock; p. 29 Dana Baldwin/iStock/Thinkstock; p. 30 Elisabeth Pollaert Smith/Photographer's Choice RF/Getty Images.

Library of Congress Cataloging-in-Publication Data

Bartley, Niccole.
 The west coast / by Niccole Bartley. — First edition
     pages cm. — (Land that I love: Regions of the United States)
 Includes index.
 ISBN 978-1-4777-6845-7 (library binding) — ISBN 978-1-4777-6846-4 (pbk.) —
 ISBN 978-1-4777-6633-0 (6-pack)
 1. Pacific States—Juvenile literature. I. Title.
 F851.B315 2015
 979—dc23

                                    2013048519

Manufactured in the United States of America

CPSIA Compliance Information: Batch # WS14PK9: For Further Information contact Rosen Publishing, New York, New York at 1-800-237-9932

CONTENTS

WELCOME TO THE WEST COAST!

The West Coast of the United States is made up of three states, which border the Pacific Ocean. These states are California, Oregon, and Washington. Because of the long **coastline**, people who live on the West Coast enjoy many great places to surf, swim, kayak, and fish.

The West Coast is known for its natural beauty. Crater Lake National Park, in Oregon, is one of more than 40 national parks on the West Coast. The lake fills the top of a dormant, or resting, volcano.

When people think of the West Coast, they may think of the Golden Gate Bridge in San Francisco, California. This bridge is known for its tall towers and orange color.

There are three **mountain ranges** and a desert on the West Coast. In between two of these mountain ranges are the **fertile** valleys surrounding the Puget Sound in Washington, the Willamette Valley in Oregon, and the Central Valley in California.

Many West Coast people enjoy nature and an outdoor lifestyle. There are many national parks and wilderness areas where people can go hiking, camping, skiing, and mountain biking.

FIRST HUMANS ON THE WEST COAST

The first humans who lived on the West Coast traveled there by foot from Asia over 15,000 years ago. More than 15 Native American nations settled in what is today Oregon and Washington. Food was plentiful. They used the wood from the forests to build **longhouses** and canoes.

The Paiute-Shoshone peoples likely carved these petroglyphs into the rocks of Owens Valley, California, about 8,000 years ago.

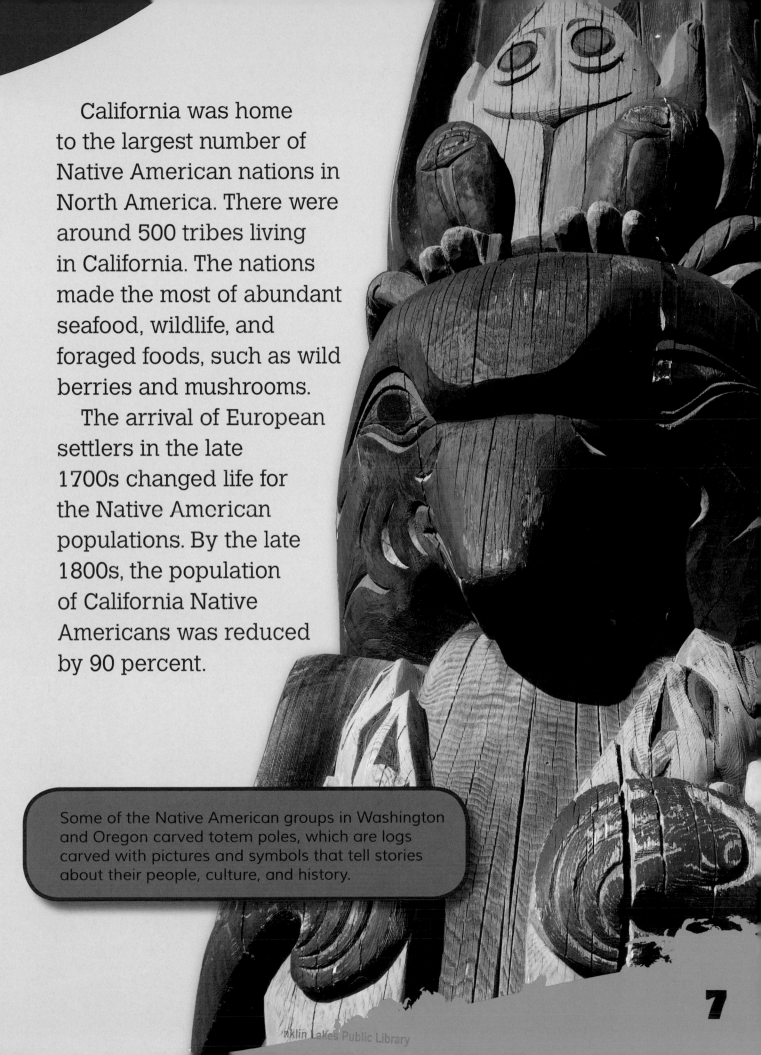

California was home to the largest number of Native American nations in North America. There were around 500 tribes living in California. The nations made the most of abundant seafood, wildlife, and foraged foods, such as wild berries and mushrooms.

The arrival of European settlers in the late 1700s changed life for the Native American populations. By the late 1800s, the population of California Native Americans was reduced by 90 percent.

Some of the Native American groups in Washington and Oregon carved totem poles, which are logs carved with pictures and symbols that tell stories about their people, culture, and history.

WEST COAST HISTORY

Beginning in the sixteenth century, English, French, Russian, and Spanish **explorers** came to the West Coast. Fur traders were the earliest European settlers there. Spain controlled most of California and built religious and military outposts, called missions, throughout the 1700s.

Sacagawea was a Shoshone woman who was married to a French fur trader. She served as Lewis and Clark's guide as they explored the Northwest Territory. She also helped other Native Americans communicate with the explorers.

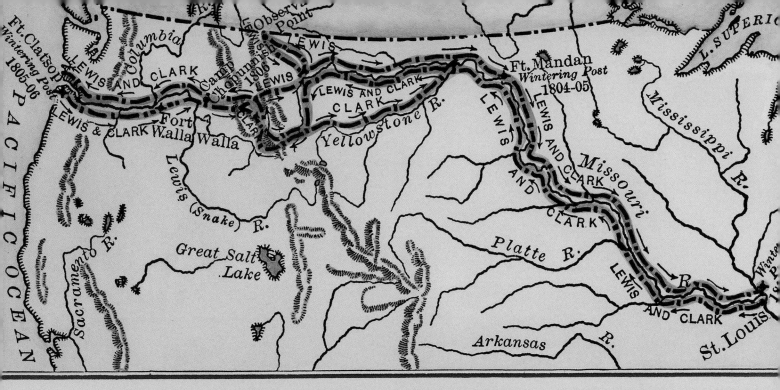

LEWIS AND CLARK EXPEDITION ROUTE

This map shows the routes the Lewis and Clark expedition took. They collected samples and made drawings of the plants, animals, and geologic features they saw along the way.

In 1805, the young US government sent the explorers Meriwether Lewis and William Clark to the West Coast. This is now known as the Lewis and Clark expedition. Lewis and Clark crossed the United States on horseback. There were no roads or trains, only trails. They arrived at the West Coast at a spot by the Columbia River, between Oregon and Washington.

By the 1830s, logging, fishing, and mining jobs attracted many settlers from the eastern United States to the West Coast. These settlers traveled west in covered wagons on a network of wagon trails. The most famous of these trails is called the Oregon Trail. More than 400,000 settlers traveled the 2,000-mile (3,200 km) Oregon Trail. It was a difficult journey and many died on the trip. Those that made it settled in many different places along the West Coast.

In 1848, gold was found in a riverbed at Sutter's Mill in Coloma, California. The gold rush began. More than 300,000 **prospectors** rushed to California to find gold. Though most of these men never found gold, California's population grew by 100,000 people.

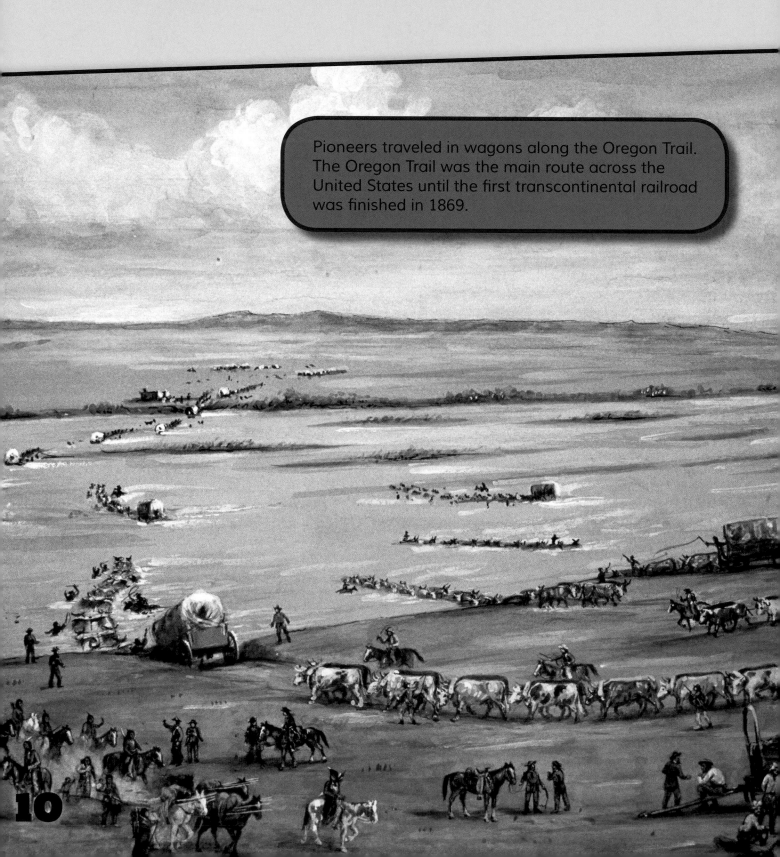

Pioneers traveled in wagons along the Oregon Trail. The Oregon Trail was the main route across the United States until the first transcontinental railroad was finished in 1869.

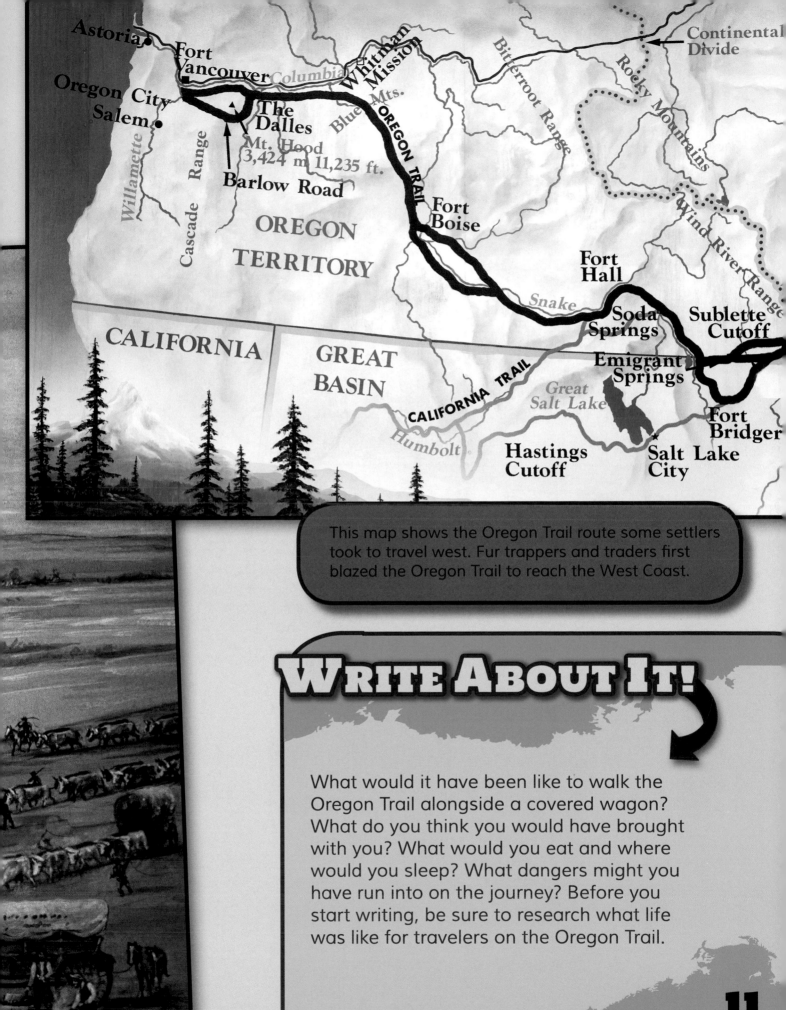

Astoria
Fort Vancouver
Columbia
Whitman Mission
Continental Divide
Oregon City
Salem
The Dalles
Barlow Road
Mt. Hood
3,424 m 11,235 ft.
Blue Mts.
OREGON TRAIL
Bitterroot Range
Rocky Mountains
Willamette
Cascade Range
OREGON TERRITORY
Fort Boise
Wind River Range
CALIFORNIA
GREAT BASIN
Snake
Fort Hall
Soda Springs
Sublette Cutoff
CALIFORNIA TRAIL
Emigrant Springs
Great Salt Lake
Fort Bridger
Humbolt
Hastings Cutoff
Salt Lake City

This map shows the Oregon Trail route some settlers took to travel west. Fur trappers and traders first blazed the Oregon Trail to reach the West Coast.

WRITE ABOUT IT!

What would it have been like to walk the Oregon Trail alongside a covered wagon? What do you think you would have brought with you? What would you eat and where would you sleep? What dangers might you have run into on the journey? Before you start writing, be sure to research what life was like for travelers on the Oregon Trail.

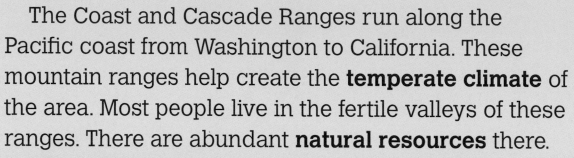

The Coast and Cascade Ranges run along the Pacific coast from Washington to California. These mountain ranges help create the **temperate climate** of the area. Most people live in the fertile valleys of these ranges. There are abundant **natural resources** there.

The Sierra Nevada forms the eastern border of California. This range has many famous national forests and wilderness areas, such as Yosemite, Sequoia National Park, and Lake Tahoe.

People enjoy hiking in the mountain ranges on the West Coast. Here a hiker has stopped to take in the view during a hike in the Cascade Range in Washington.

The Sierra Nevada is 400 miles (640 km) long and about 70 miles (110 km) across.

The West Coast rests on three shifting **plates** below Earth's surface. The meeting of the two larger plates is called the San Andreas Fault. The shifting plates cause earthquakes. People on the West Coast have adapted to these natural disasters. They have learned to build stronger houses. They also have emergency plans in place to help people get out of the cities and towns safely.

SAN ANDREAS FAULT

The San Andreas Fault runs through the city of San Francisco. In 1906, there was a major earthquake in the city. It was one of the worst natural disasters in our country's history. More than 3,000 people died, and much of the city was destroyed.

DESERTS AND FORESTS

The West Coast is home to many wonderful natural areas. Sequoia National Park is a remarkable forest of sequoia trees. Some of the largest and oldest trees in the world are found there.

The West Coast also has temperate rain forests, including the Hoh Rain Forest, in Olympic National Park in Washington. Annual rainfall amounts to 140 to 170 inches (356–432 cm), or 12 to 14 feet (3.7–4.3 m), each year!

Death Valley is the lowest, hottest, and driest place in North America.

Here a mother and her child check out a giant cedar tree in the Hoh Rain Forest.

Southern California is home to the Mojave Desert. Death Valley National Park, in the Mojave, is the lowest point in North America. There is very little rainfall in the Mojave, only about 2 inches (5 cm) a year! Plants and animals that live in the Mojave have adapted to live with very little water.

MORE ON THE MOJAVE

The northern parts of the Mojave are cold, while the southern parts are very hot. There are dune fields in the desert. Some of the dunes reach 600 feet (183 m) high. The desert is home to scrub trees, such as the Joshua tree, that are not found anywhere else in the world.

15

THE WEST COAST

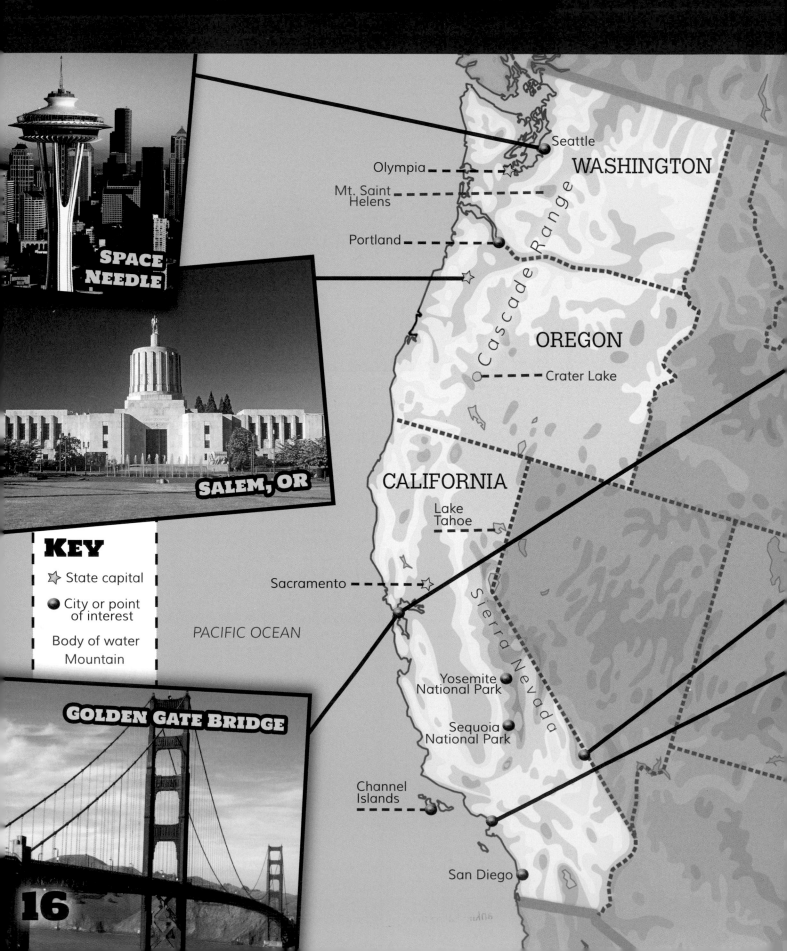

SPACE NEEDLE

SALEM, OR

KEY

☆ State capital

● City or point of interest

Body of water
Mountain

GOLDEN GATE BRIDGE

Seattle

Olympia

Mt. Saint Helens

Portland

WASHINGTON

Cascade Range

OREGON

Crater Lake

CALIFORNIA

Lake Tahoe

Sacramento

Sierra Nevada

PACIFIC OCEAN

Yosemite National Park

Sequoia National Park

Channel Islands

San Diego

TROLLEY

SAN FRANCISCO, CA

MOJAVE DESERT, DEATH VALLEY

LOS ANGELES, CA

HOLLYWOOD SIGN

HOLLYWOOD

WEST COAST PLANTS AND ANIMALS

The West Coast has 34 national forests and huge areas of protected wilderness. Many different plants and animals live in these **habitats**, including black bears, coyotes, bobcats, beavers, wolves, bighorn sheep, and moose. Hundreds of rare insects, such as glow-in-the-dark millipedes, can be found nowhere else on the planet.

Fur seals and sea lions live on the West Coast, too. They are **marine mammals** with flippers. They hunt for fish in the Pacific Ocean. Sea lions can be found barking in large groups on piers in San Francisco Bay.

Pier 39 in San Francisco has become famous for the hundreds of sea lions that haul out at certain times of year. Pier 39 is also known for its restaurants, entertainers, and aquarium.

Here you can see mosses growing all over this natural archway in the Hoh Rain Forest.

Many kinds of plants do well in the warm, humid climate. There are tiny mosses and giant trees. The Douglas fir, western hemlock, coast redwoods, Sitka spruce, and western red cedar are plentiful.

THE CALIFORNIA CONDOR

The California condor is North America's largest bird. Condors are vultures. A vulture is a bird that eats animal **carcasses**. They have a wingspan of nearly 10 feet (3 m). The California condor travels over 140 miles (225 km) each day to find food.

The California condor is a symbol of wilderness. Native American cultures believed that these birds could give humans special powers. Tribal leaders wore condor feathers to help them find lost people or things.

The West Coast region has many natural resources that have shaped its **economy**. California has one of the largest economies in the world. California farmers grow most of the fruits and vegetables in the United States. They also make the most wine, milk, and cheese. California is home to many technology companies as well.

Washington's many forests have led the state to become a leading lumber producer. Washington companies also build airplanes and ships. Agriculture is a big part of the economy, too. Washington has many orchards and grows beans and potatoes. Farmers also raise animals for meat and wool. Fishing is a big industry in Washington, especially salmon fishing.

Tourism is an important source of income for all of the West Coast states. People come to ski on the mountains, visit the cities, and enjoy the other sights the West Coast has to offer.

One of California's major industries is grape growing. The grapes are used for table grapes and to make raisins, vinegar, juice, and wines. California is the fourth-largest wine-producing region in the world.

Oregon also produces a lot of lumber and wood products. Much of Oregon's ample farmland is used to grow hay for livestock, as well as other crops.

The West Coast is home to many technology companies, such as Microsoft, which has its headquarters in Redmond, Washington.

Coastal states often have large **seaports**. This is certainly true of the West Coast. Los Angeles, in Southern California, is the second-largest US city after New York City. Los Angeles is home to Hollywood, the entertainment capital of the world.

San Diego is about 120 miles (190 km) south of Los Angeles and is the second-largest city in California. Tourism is a big industry in San Diego because of its excellent climate and many beaches.

Olympia is a city in Washington that sits on the banks of Budd Inlet, the southernmost arm of Puget Sound. People who live there enjoy fishing, sailing, and many activities that take advantage of the waterside location.

Portland, Oregon, is the major port city in Oregon. It sits on the banks of two rivers, the Willamette and Columbia Rivers. The Columbia gives it access to the Pacific Ocean.

San Francisco, in Northern California, is one of the most-visited cities in the world. It is known for its cool summers, fog, and steep hills.

Portland, Oregon, has worked hard to become an **environmentally friendly** city. Seattle, Washington, is known for its green industries, too. It is also known for being rainy and for its coffee shops.

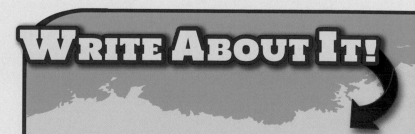

WRITE ABOUT IT!

Choose a West Coast city to research. Pretend you are visiting that city and write a postcard home talking about what you did there.

23

SEEING THE SIGHTS!

Seattle's Space Needle has a rotating restaurant and an observation deck from which to take in the city views. The antenna on top makes the building 605 feet (184 m) tall.

There are many famous man-made landmarks on the West Coast. When people think about the West Coast, they often think of San Francisco's Golden Gate Bridge or the Space Needle in Seattle. San Francisco is also known for its beautiful rows of Victorian homes and the cable cars riding up and down the steep hills.

Every city and town has its own important places, but the West Coast as a region is best known for its spectacular beaches and coastlines and the many beautiful national parks. The most famous parks are Yosemite, Redwood National Park, Joshua Tree National Park, Crater Lake, the Channel Islands, Mount Rainier, and Olympic National Park.

Many people visit the California missions while they are in the state. The missions, such as San Luis Rey, shown here, were military and religious outposts built by the Spanish when they were settling the area.

WEST COAST CULTURE

The West Coast is filled with many natural wonders. This is part of what makes it a very special place in our country. Dating back to the earliest settlers, people of the West Coast have worked together to save the natural beauty of the wilderness. The Sierra Club is a **conservation** group in the United States. John Muir created the Sierra Club in 1892. He had a vision to create Yosemite National Park and preserve many other special places on the West Coast. Today, people on the West Coast enjoy an outdoor lifestyle that celebrates these protected areas.

Many people who live in the waterfront city of Seattle enjoy sailing in Puget Sound. Seattle is also known for its music and its coffee shops.

Oregon has large areas of orchard and farmland. People can tour the orchards and even pick their own apples or pears.

The discovery of gold in California turned San Francisco into a bustling city full of new arrivals. They came from different parts of the country and the world, especially Asia and Europe. All these new people brought their own traditions and foods with them. These flavors, from sourdough bread to sushi, are still part of the West Coast diet. Settlers planted fruit orchards and grapevines in the hills beyond the cities. The area is still known for these fruits. People come from all over the world to tour the vineyards and orchards of the West Coast.

The rush of settlers to the West Coast also brought about many new technologies, including the construction of railroads. The entrepreneurial spirit that brought immigrants and settlers to the West Coast continues to be part of the region's culture. The West Coast leads the country in technology and many other industries.

Yosemite's many scenic views, waterfalls, and challenging hiking trails bring locals and tourists alike outdoors to explore and enjoy the natural beauty of the park.

Marina del Rey is a village in Los Angeles. It is the largest man-made small craft harbor and can hold more than 5,000 boats. Surrounding the harbor are places to live, eat, watch music, and more.

REGIONAL RECIPES:
MAKE A SMOOTHIE

The West Coast, and especially California, is famous for its fresh fruits and vegetables. The region has also brought us many great recipes that are now popular all over the country. Try to make your own fruit smoothie!

INGREDIENTS:
4 cups strawberries (remove green stem)
1 banana, broken into chunks
1 cup orange juice
2 cups ice

DIRECTIONS:
In a blender, combine strawberries and bananas. Blend until fruit is pureed. Blend in the juice. Add ice and blend until smooth. Pour into glasses and serve.

WE LOVE THE WEST COAST!

The West Coast of North America is home to some of the largest and most important cities and industries in the world. It has also impacted American culture through its food, music, technology, and entertainment.

Many people enjoy living in and visiting the West Coast. They are drawn by the beauty of the Pacific coastline, the temperate climate, and the region's diverse geography.

In addition to the breathtaking natural landscape, there are so many beautiful, man-made, and historic landmarks and sights to see on the West Coast. Here San Francisco's famous Painted Ladies, which are colorful Victorian row houses, can be seen against the city skyline.

GLOSSARY

carcasses (KAHR-kus-ez) Dead bodies.

climate (KLY-mut) The kind of weather a certain area has.

coastline (KOHST-lyn) The land alongside the sea.

conservation (kon-sur-VAY-shun) Protecting something from harm.

economy (ih-KAH-nuh-mee) The way in which a country or a business oversees its goods and services.

environmentally friendly (in-vy-run-MENT-tul-ee FREND-lee) Not likely to hurt the natural world.

explorers (ek-SPLOR-erz) People who travel and look for new land.

fertile (FER-tul) Good for making and growing things.

habitats (HA-buh-tats) The kinds of land where animals or plants naturally live.

longhouses (LONG-hows-ez) Long, narrow, single-room buildings made by certain Native American groups.

marine mammals (muh-REEN MA-mulz) Warm-blooded animals that have backbones and hair, breathe air, and feed milk to their young and live or spend much of their time in the ocean.

mountain ranges (MOWN-tun RAYNJ-ez) Series of mountains. Two or more mountain ranges together form a mountain system.

natural resources (NA-chuh-rul REE-sors-ez) Things in nature that can be used by people.

plates (PLAYTS) The moving pieces of Earth's crust, the top layer of Earth.

prospectors (PRAH-spek-terz) People who explore areas for minerals, such as gold.

seaports (SEE-ports) Coastal places where boats can dock to load or unload cargo.

temperate (TEM-puh-rut) Not too hot or too cold.

INDEX

WEBSITES

Due to the changing nature of Internet links, PowerKids Press has developed an online list of websites related to the subject of this book. This site is updated regularly. Please use this link to access the list:

www.powerkidslinks.com/ltil/westc/